Schmitz, Dorothy Childers
Muhammad Ali, the greatest

MUHAMMAD ALI

ALI

THE GREATEST

MUHAMMAD ALI

THE GREATEST

By Dorothy Childers Schmitz

Reprinted 1979

Library of Congress Catalog Card Number: 77-70893. International Standard Book Number: 0-913940-60-7.

Design - Doris Woods and Randal M. Heise

PHOTOGRAPHIC CREDITS

On a January day in 1942, a baby boy was born to Mr. and Mrs. Cassius Clay. They lived in Louisville, Kentucky. They named their baby son Cassius Clay, Jr.

Twenty-two years later, that baby would be the heavyweight champion of the world. His name would no longer be Cassius Clay. He would be called Muhammad Ali. He would also be called the greatest boxer the world has ever known.

Little Cassius Clay grew very fast. When he was only three, he could no longer sleep in his crib. One day when he was playing with his mother, he hit her in the mouth. To her surprise, a tooth was loose, and it had to be pulled!

Friends of the Clay family watched the child grow big and strong. He was always cheerful and happy. He was not a good student in school. But he could run and he could fight. Sometimes he ran beside the school bus just for fun. The children in the bus laughed. He loved to make them laugh.

Young Clay shows his Golden Gloves medal to his friend, Officer Joe Martin.

One day someone stole his bicycle. He was angry. He wanted to find his bicycle. He also wanted to punish the person who took it. He went to his friend who was a policeman. His name was Joe Martin. He asked officer Martin to help him find his bicycle. He wanted to teach the thief a lesson.

Mr. Martin tried to calm little Cassius. He told him to go to the gym and he would teach him how to fight.

Before long Cassius liked to box more than anything else. He became better and better. He trained every day. He knew he was good.

Mr. and Mrs. Clay gaze proudly at their son.

Cassius Clay in early press photo.

When Cassius was only twelve years old, he began to win fights. But he did not win many friends. The other boys at the gym did not like to hear him brag. But he kept right on telling them, "I am the greatest."

He was the greatest young boxer that officer Martin had ever seen. He could see that Cassius might really be great.

Mr. Clay was proud of his young son. One day Cassius told his father, "Daddy, I'm going to win $4,000 on the Gillette Cavalcade of Sports some day."

Soon young Cassius was fighting on TV. When he graduated from high school, he had fought 180 amateur fights. He had won Golden Gloves tournaments. His mother was not surprised at this. She told her friends, "The first thing Baby Cassius said was "Gee-Gee!" That was his way of saying, 'Golden Gloves'."

Cassius gets ready for the Olympics.

Young Clay told officer Martin of his dream to be world champion. "I know I can do it," he said.

Officer Martin gave him some good advice. He told him to try for the Olympics.

So Cassius Clay went to Rome for the 1960 Olympics. He had just graduated from high school in Louisville. And here he was on his way to the Olympics!

At the Olympics, he fought for the first time without Officer Martin in his corner. But he won! Now he really did feel that he could be a winner. He even shouted to Floyd Patterson in the crowd, "Floyd Patterson, I'm going to whup you some day. I am the greatest." Floyd Patterson smiled and said, "You're a good kid, keep trying, kid."

Cassius fights a Russian boxer during the Olympic trials.

Clay flew home from the Olympics with his gold medal. People began to believe that he really was the greatest. He was their hero.

Soon Cassius Clay would become a pro boxer. He was eighteen years old. He was six feet two inches tall and he weighed over 200 pounds. He was quick and strong.

Everywhere he went he told people, "I am the greatest!" Many people did not like him because of the things he said. But many people liked him anyway. They could see that he was right.

Back in Louisville some friends told his mother, "He shouldn't brag so much." She said, "He started to talk at the age of ten months. And that's pretty early for a boy."

People everywhere began to hear more and more about Cassius Clay. They heard about his boxing. And they heard about the things he was saying about himself and other fighters. He became famous for poems he made up about his fights. Some people called him the "Louisville Lip."

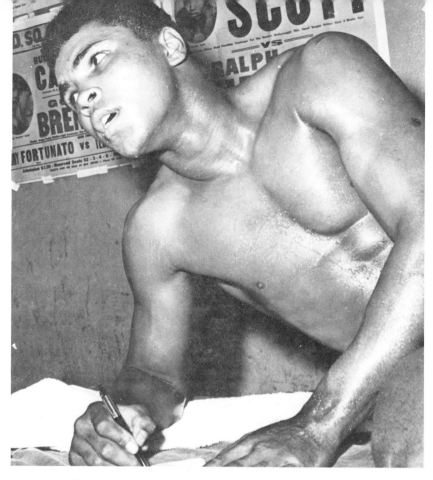

Clay writes one of his poems before a fight.

He had something to say about the people who did not like him. He said, "Now you take a dog, he can bark at the moon all night, but the moon is so high and so remote that it never replies to the dog." He did not seem to care that everyone did not like him. He vowed that they would someday know that he was a great boxer.

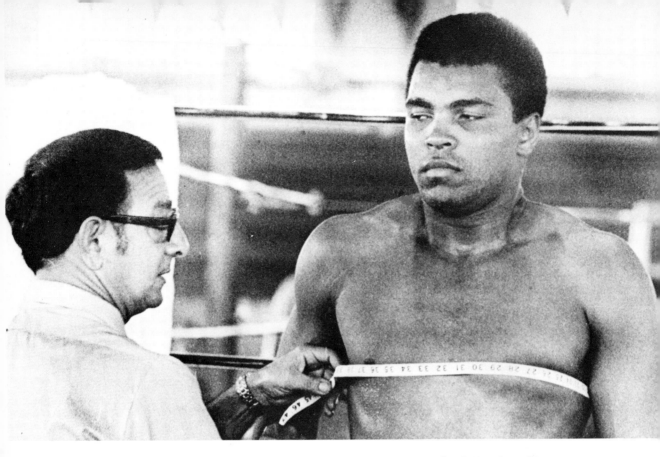

Angleo Dundee has remained the manager and friend of Cassius (later Muhammad) all through the boxer's career.

Now Cassius Clay was going to be a pro boxer. He had to find a trainer to help him. A man named Angelo Dundee became his trainer. Mr. Dundee was glad to be his trainer. He knew that Clay did not drink or smoke. He knew he would train hard. He knew they would make a lot of money.

Clay won his first fight as a pro. After six rounds he was called the winner. Clay kept fighting and he kept winning. He would tell people that he would win in a certain round. And he would. He won his first fifteen fights as a pro. But the fighters he defeated were not so well-known as he was. He wanted to fight someone really famous.

In his Olympic trunks, Clay fights his first pro fight.

In November, 1962, he got his chance. He was going to fight Archie Moore. Moore was an ex-champion. But Clay was sure he could win. He made up a poem:

"When you come to the fight
Don't block aisle or door,
Cause Archie Moore
Will fall in four!"

It happened! Moore went down in four!

Archie Moore falls in four!

Now Clay wanted to fight the world champ. People all over the world had watched him fight Moore on TV. They believed him when he said he was great. But some people wanted to see him lose. They wanted someone to "Shut his mouth." Others did not care that he bragged. They wanted to see him win.

Clay kept winning fights. He kept making fun of the champ. He wanted to fight Sonny

Clay fights Sonny Liston for the heavyweight title.

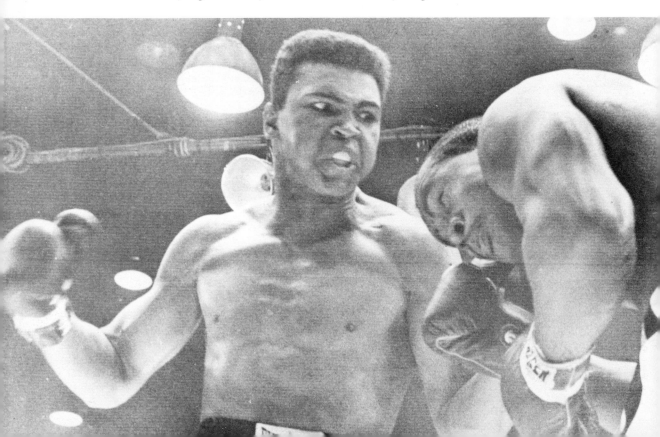

Liston. Then he would be the champ. Liston had been undefeated for nine years.

Not many people thought Clay could beat Liston. But Clay thought he could.

In February, 1964, he got his chance. He fought Liston in Miami Beach. He won the match in six rounds. Cassius Clay was the World's Heavyweight Champion! And he was only twenty-two years old.

Bundini Brown and Angelo Dundee celebrate with the new World Heavyweight Champion!

Everyone was talking about the young champion. Some thought there was magic about him. He could do things that other boxers could not do. They said he had some kind of radar. He could tell when a punch was coming. People wanted to know if he could take a punch. But nobody could hit him! He was too quick.

Clay joins his brother Rudolph, Malcolm X and the ambassador from Nigeria in an interview.

The day after the fight, Cassius Clay shocked the world again. But this time it was not a fight. He told the world, "I believe in the religion of Islam. I believe there is no God but Allah."

Now Cassius Clay would be a Black Muslim. He would have to give up his name. It was hard for him to do this. He had always been proud of his name. He had made it famous. But he believed in the religion of Islam. And it was what he had to do. His new name would be Muhammad Ali.

This news was a shock to many people. They thought this action would hurt his boxing career. Black Muslims did not like white people. They believed that black people could get along without help from white people. Many people thought the new champ should be thankful to white people. They believed that whites had helped him achieve his goal. The new champ did not think so.

Many people who had liked him before did not like him now. They wanted him to lose. But he kept winning. He defeated Sonny Liston again the next year.

It was 1966. The United States was involved in a war in Viet Nam. Young men were being sent there to fight. People were asking, "Why doesn't Ali have to go to fight in the war?" He said he could not go to war because of his religion. He was told to report to the Army. He would not go. Now he was in great trouble. Still he would not go. Because of this, boxing officials took away his heavyweight crown. It looked as if he might never fight again. But he would not give in.

There was a trial to decide if Ali was a draft evader. It went on for a long time. Ali did not know what they would decide.

He could not fight, but he could still talk. He went around to colleges. He told people that the Viet Nam war was wrong.

In 1967, Ali married a girl named Belinda Boyd. She was a Black Muslim, too. Her new name was Khalilah. The next year a little girl was born. They named her Maryum.

In 1970, there was another trial. This time they decided that Ali could fight again. But it had been three years since his last fight.

He fought Jerry Quarry in October, 1970. The fight was in Atlanta, Georgia. People were happy to see Ali back in the ring. He did not brag about his fight. He seemed different. Ali also looked different in the ring. He was not as fast. But he did win.

Ali returns to the ring.

Ali's next fight was with Oscar Bonavena. This man had never been defeated. But Ali felt like himself again. He said he could win. Ali fought hard, and after fifteen rounds, he had won.

Ali felt good again. Now he had his eye on a goal. He wanted to be the champ again. The man he would have to beat was Joe Frazier.

This was the fight the world was waiting to see. People called it "The Fight of the Century."

Frazier was younger than Ali. He had many fans. Ali had won back many of his fans. He began to make up poems again. He wrote this one about Joe Frazier:

"Joe's gonna come out smoking,
And I ain't gonna be joking,
I'll be pecking and a poking,
Pouring water on his smoking.
This might shock and amaze ya,
But I'm gonna retire Joe Frazier!"

The fight was in Madison Square Garden in New York. It was March, 1971. There were 20,000 people there. Many more were watching on TV.

Frazier fights hard to keep his title.

People cheered when Frazier came out. But they went wild when Ali came out. The fight began. Ali looked good for five rounds. Then he began to slow down. Frazier was able to connect some of his punches. That made Ali work harder. Then he seemed to be winning. Both fighters were tired. In round fifteen Frazier knocked Ali down. He got up. But Ali had lost. Joe Frazier was still champ.

Now Ali knew that he would have to work harder. He would have to train harder. He would have to fight other fights. Then he could try again to get back the title.

Ali won his next ten fights. Then something very surprising happened. In March, 1973, Ali fought Ken Norton. Norton was not famous yet. People thought Ali would win. But Norton broke Ali's jaw.

Ali falls to Frazier in round fifteen.

Famous people like Sammy Davis, Jr. admire Ali.

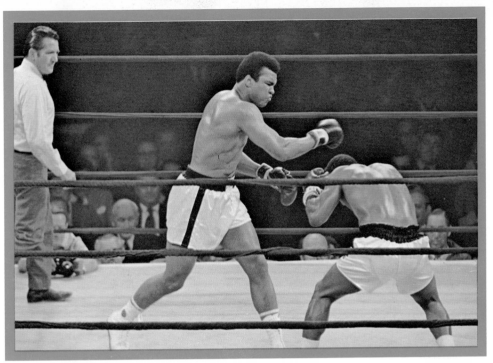
Muhammad Ali fights his way back to the top.

Now many people thought Ali's boxing career was over. They had been wearing buttons that said "The People's Champ." Some people tried to turn them in. They thought it was the end of Muhammad Ali!

But they were wrong. Ali wanted to show them. And he wanted to show Norton. Ali's broken jaw mended. His trainer Dundee said his jaw was better than ever. Ali said, "I gave Norton glory. Now I have to punish him."

Ali got his chance in September, 1973. He fought Ken Norton in Los Angeles. After twelve rounds, Ali won.

Now he wanted to fight Joe Frazier again. But he would not be fighting for the title this time. Frazier had lost his title to George Foreman. Ali won the match with Frazier this time.

Now he was ready to fight for the title again. Ali worked hard. He wanted to be champ again. He knew he could do it.

All through 1974, he trained hard at his camp in Pennsylvania. He did his road work and shadow boxing. Another thing he liked to do to keep in shape was chop wood. He said, "I took my strength from the trees."

Ali trains hard for the title match.

Meeting reporters before the African fight, Ali shouts, "I am the greatest!"

Many people wanted him to get the title back. Some people thought that he had never lost it.

Others wanted him to lose. They still hated his bragging. They wanted him out of boxing.

Now this fight was being called "The Fight of the Century." It would be fought in Africa in the new nation of Zaire. People all over the world waited to see this fight. More than a billion people would be watching by television satellite.

"I am the greatest."

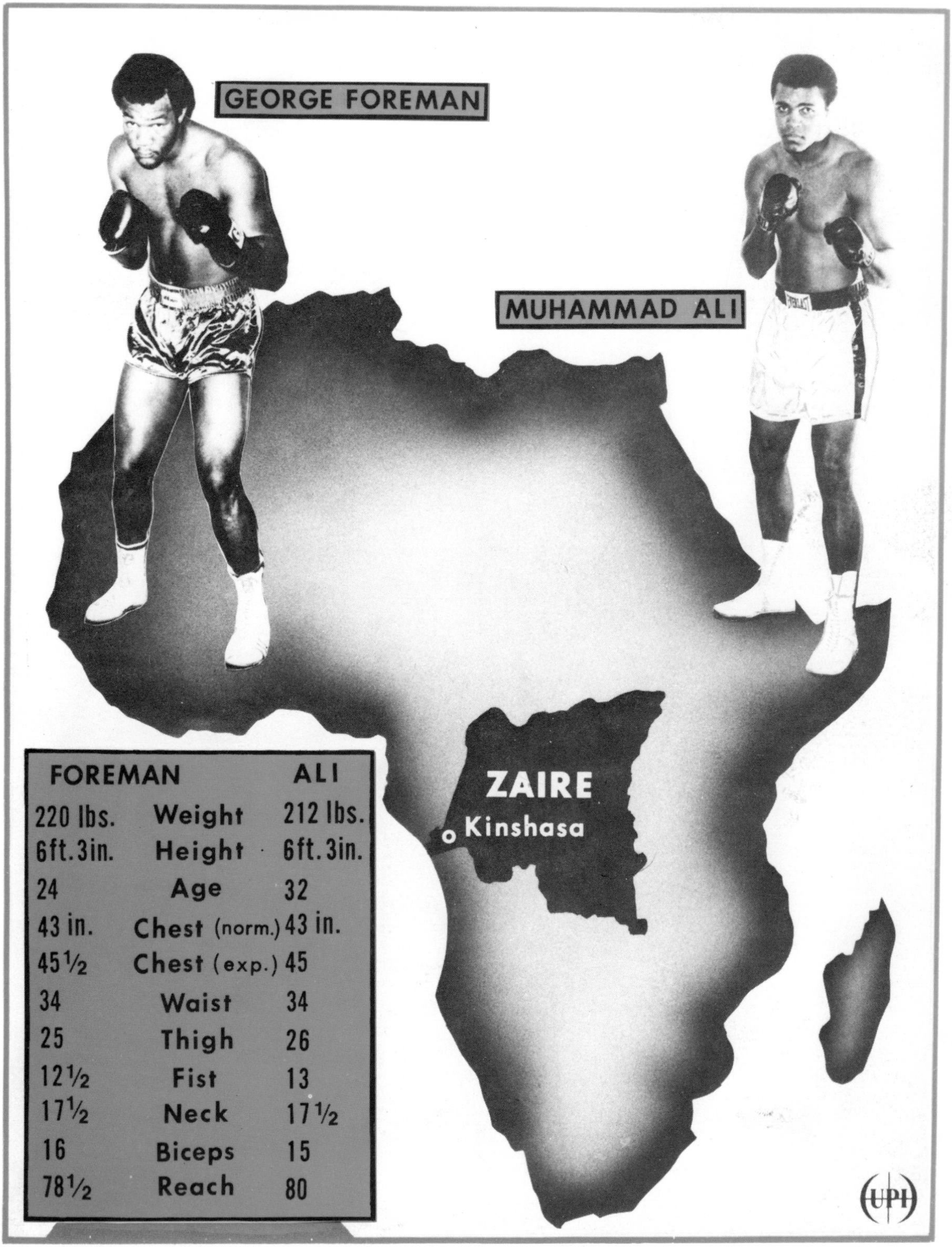

GEORGE FOREMAN

MUHAMMAD ALI

ZAIRE

o Kinshasa

FOREMAN		ALI
220 lbs.	Weight	212 lbs.
6 ft. 3 in.	Height	6 ft. 3 in.
24	Age	32
43 in.	Chest (norm.)	43 in.
45½	Chest (exp.)	45
34	Waist	34
25	Thigh	26
12½	Fist	13
17½	Neck	17½
16	Biceps	15
78½	Reach	80

UPI

35

Foreman's people felt good about their man. Archie Moore said Ali would be ruined.

Ali's people felt good, too. They said Ali would be the champ again. Ali said, "When all is said and did and done, George Foreman will fall in one."

George Foreman weighs in before the fight in Zaire.

It was one of the greatest fights in boxing history. It was 4:00 A.M. and 60,000 people were in the stadium.

Ali was different. Foreman thought he would dance and move the way he always did. But he didn't. Even his people asked him between rounds, "Why don't you dance?" "You got to dance." Ali answered, "Don't talk. I know what I'm doing."

All through the first eight rounds, Foreman tried hard to land a good punch. He began to wear out. Then Ali went to work. He knocked Foreman down. Ali had done it. He had regained the title!

Now he was champ again. Every fighter wanted a chance to fight him. The next year, he fought and won against Chuck Wepner, Ron Lyle, and Joe Bugner. It looked as if the title was his to keep.

But there was one fighter who wanted a third chance at Ali. It was Joe Frazier.

It was September, 1975. The fight was in Manila. Ali had to be serious. Frazier did his very best for fourteen rounds. Then he was finished. Ali was still the champ.

Ali waits as Foreman is counted out.

After that fight, Ali said, "I'll tell the world right now, Joe Frazier brings out the best in me."

Ali fought often in 1976. Every young fighter wanted a chance to fight the champ. They thought he was getting old. They wanted a chance to win the title.

In April, he fought Jimmy Young in Landover, Maryland. Ali weighed 230 pounds. This was the most he had ever weighed in a match. He did not fight as vigorously as he had in other fights. But Young was not good enough. Ali won after fifteen rounds.

Ken Norton was at that fight. He cheered Ali on. He wanted another chance at the title.

After the fight, Ali said, "People want life and death all the time from me. Let me have a little rest."

Now everyone began to talk about the fight between Norton and Ali. It would take place in the fall. They wondered if Norton could break Ali's jaw again. They wondered if Ali was too old. He was thirty-four years old.

Ali fights to keep his title.

The fight was held at Yankee Stadium. A record crowd was there to watch. It was September 28, 1976. This fight was so close that after fifteen rounds, people could not guess who was winning. After the fight was over, both fighters waited in their corners. Norton waited with high hopes that he had won. Ali waited and worried that he had not won. Two judges scored the fight 8-7 for Ali. The referee called it 8-6-1. Ali was still champ! But it had been close.

Many newsmen thought Norton may have won. Ali himself explained it this way:

"To beat a champion, you got to BEAT him. You can't fight like Jimmy Young or Norton. You got to convince people you won. You got to whip the champion, just like I did to Foreman. You got to whip him."

Three days after the fight, Ali flew to Istanbul, Turkey. He met with leaders of his religious faith. They told him to retire. He told newsmen, "As of now I am quitting boxing and will devote all my energy to the Moslem faith."

The next week he was in Miami Beach with movie producers. They were making a film called "The Greatest." It would be the story of Ali's life. News reporters asked him, "Are you going to retire?" He did not answer.

But Ali did not retire. During the next year, Ali fought Norton again. Norton was still a strong fighter. He wanted the title. But Ali was not about to give it up. Ali won. But the fans could see that he was not as fast as he was when he was younger.

Another boxer who tried to take the crown away in 1977 was Ernie Shavers. During the first few rounds, it looked as if he might beat Ali. Then Ali went at Shavers like the young Ali. After Ali had won, Dundee said to him, "I don't know how you do it, but I love you for it."

But that fight had taken something out of Ali. In his dressing room, he said to Dundee, "I'm tired. I'm so tired. I'm through. I don't need anyone else to tell me." Dundee said to reporters, "He has to make up his own mind."

But Ali was not through. The next year, a young man named Leon Spinks wanted a shot at the champ. In February, 1978, he got his chance.

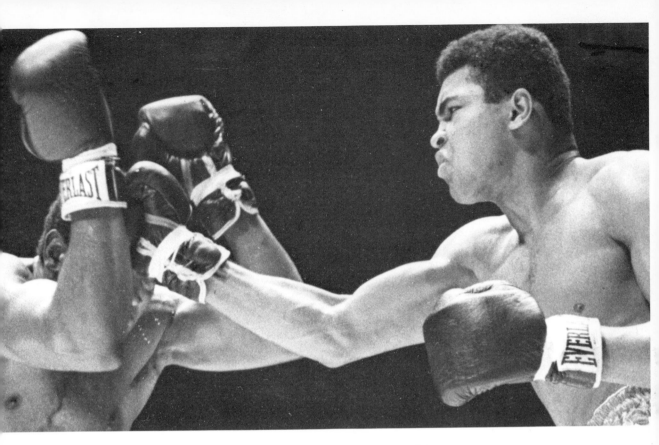
Ken Norton tries to take the title.

In Las Vegas, young Spinks beat Ali in a split decision fight. Spinks was the new heavy-weight champion.

Ali took it like a man. After the fight he said to reporters, "I lost fair and square to Spinks. I lost because Spinks was better, that's all."

Even Spinks said, "I'm the best young heavyweight but not the greatest. He's the greatest."

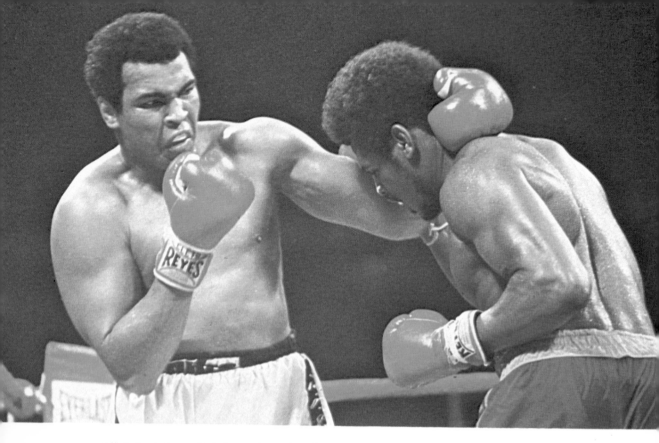

Ali defeats Leon Spinks and regains the heavyweight championship for a record third time.

The world waited to see what the great Ali would do. He had captured the title twice. Would he be the first ever to win the crown three times?

They did not have to wait long. After a rest, Ali began to train again. He knew it would not be easy. He was thirty-six years old, and he had to beat the twenty-four-year-old champ to get the title back.

He ran until his lungs burned and his tongue was swollen. He did more than eight thousand push-ups. "I hated every minute of it," he said. But he said to himself, "Suffer now, and live the rest of your life as a champion."

And that is just what he did. Only 212 days after he had lost the championship to Spinks, he won it back again. It was September in the Superdome in New Orleans. He looked like the young Ali again. He danced. He used his hands. He was in control. Ali was thirty-six years old. And he had won the title three times.

On June 26, 1979, Ali resigned his title. He had announced his retirement before. But he had never before made it official. This time it was official. He wrote a letter to the World Boxing Association. He told reporters, "I'm thirty-seven. That's a record for heavyweights. I'm the three-time champion. That's the best way to be remembered."

Angelo Dundee said, "We'll never see another one like him."

If You Enjoyed

MUHAMMAD ALI
THE GREATEST

Then Don't Miss Reading

FRAN TARKENTON
MASTER OF THE GRIDIRON

O. J. SIMPSON
THE JUICE IS LOOSE

CHRIS EVERT
WOMEN'S TENNIS CHAMPION

EVEL KNIEVEL
MOTORCYCLE DAREDEVIL

DOROTHY HAMILL
SKATE TO VICTORY

from

CRESTWOOD HOUSE

P.O. BOX 3427   MANKATO, MINNESOTA 56001

Write Us for a Complete Catalog